The Last ADl RECOVERY Guide

The Infallible Method To Overcome Any Addiction

Table of Contents:

Introduction

I want to thank you and congratulate you for downloading the book, "The Last ADDICTION RECOVERY Guide: The Easiest Way To Finally Overcome Any Addiction".

This book contains proven steps and strategies on how to understand your addiction problems, help your loved ones with their struggle against their compulsions, and devise the recovery methods that would work best for you. At the same time, this book will also serve as your guide in making your personal goals for the sake of overcoming addiction.

Addiction is as bad as cancer. Nobody ever wanted to be dependent on something, and they never meant to become dependent. This is the very first thing you need to understand about this state of living. You must condition your mind first and remove any kind of stigma that comes with the term "addiction." Several factors come into play when people are led into this demise, and it's never because they are weak-willed. To help an addict or yourself, this is the very first thing you need to get a full grasp on.

Everyone has dreams and so do these people. It just so happens that the circumstances in their lives led them to this state of living. And just because they have become seemingly mindless zombies who could only function properly when they had a shot of their addiction, it doesn't necessarily make their lives worthless. They are as sentient as the person next to them, and this means they have every chance to recover.

Keep in mind that every time you conduct an intervention, you save a person from the possibility of landing on the streets, begging for food and money, and seeking another chance at redemption.

Therefore, if you are suffering from addiction, or you know someone who does, this is the book you need to read. Not only will this book help you understand your true struggles and how you can help yourself, it would also guide you towards making the right personal decisions and address the situation. This book would provide you all the things that you need in order for you to personalize your strategies to help yourself or your loved one defeat compulsions such as substance abuse, gambling problems, shopping addiction, or binge eating.

Thanks again for downloading this book, I hope you enjoy it!

Chapter 1: Understanding the Enemy

When people hear the word "addiction" they automatically think substance abuse, such as excessive drinking and smoking or taking illegal drugs. However, addiction actually has a much wider coverage.

Addiction, in reality, is not just about the condition that a person experiences when he ingests a substance and then he eventually could not stop. Addiction is doing or taking anything to the point that this activity interferes with the most ordinary activities. Those suffering from addiction realize that doing that particular activity does them harm but they cannot stop.

Types of Addiction

With that said, a clearer picture needs to be drawn to get a better understanding of a person's situation. To start, know that there are two categories of addiction, and below them are the several types and substances – some even deemed harmless by many – that stand as the foundation of problems for an individual.

There are **substance-related addictions**, and as many commonly know, these include drugs and alcohol. Contrary to popular knowledge, however, included in this list is a seemingly innocent substance.

1. *Street drugs*
    This is the most popular form of addiction. Topping the list of most abused illegal substances are meth, cocaine, and GHB, but of course, there are several others that follow.

There are several misconceptions about drug addiction, however. First off, many are of the belief that as long as a person has tried it – even just once – he already belongs in the addicts club. This is technically incorrect. A person can only be properly categorized as an addict if he begins to abuse the substance. Another myth about drugs is that it only takes one try for a person to get hooked. As pointed out throughout this book, addiction is a psychological disorder. That means, despite the curiosity, as long as an individual has complete control over his life, he is not bound to automatically adopt this destructive habit.

Despite these myths, however, you should understand that the use of drugs is illegal regardless of the number of uses. A person can get incarcerated for showing signs of use, or being caught with a pack.

2. *Alcohol*
Among the list of substance addictions, alcoholism holds the top rank. Since alcohol has been the constant companion of most forms of socialization, distinguishing social from abusive drinking has become a challenge for most experts. To top it off, there is no single determining factor to spark this. In essence, anyone from anywhere, rich or poor, is prone to becoming an alcoholic.

One common sign of alcoholism – although not exclusively – is if a person seeks the comfort of liquor instead of friends when encountering difficulties, or any form of negativity, in their life. An individual who drinks at inappropriate times, such as in the morning or at work, may be edging towards the habit.

Many believe that the effects of alcohol are temporary – that a person will experience physical and mental changes exclusively during its presence in the body. This is true for moderate drinkers. When the substance is being abused, however, the changes become permanent, damaging, and even fatal—similar to how illegal drugs affect the body.

3. *Tobacco*
Next to alcohol is tobacco addiction. Unlike the former, however, smoking has been one of the leading causes of illness and death all over the globe. As many came to know, the primary substance that makes smoking addictive is nicotine. Basically, what makes it so is the adrenaline rush it helps the body release, and the amount of dopamine it aids in increasing. If adrenaline gives the body a boost in physical and mental energy and functionality, dopamine triggers "happiness" and "pleasure." This is one of the reasons why smokers light a cigarette whenever they feel stressed or panicked. Furthermore, it is not only through smoking can tobacco become addictive and lethal. Some forms of it can be chewed, but it will give the person the same effects and risks.

Some people argue that a person is not a tobacco addict if he only chooses to smoke in certain occasions or for a set number of times a day instead of out of impulse. Technically, however, society and experts view this habit in a black and white manner. A person is either a smoker or not, and should he belong in the former, then he will be automatically deemed an addict.

Despite the fact the nicotine has addictive properties, trying smoking once wouldn't make a person an instant smoker. Again, addiction is a psychological battle. There are those who claim to have tried a stick or two but found no reason to make smoking an everyday habit.

4. *Prescription drugs*
Pharmaceutical drugs were developed for good reasons and beneficial purposes, but when a person uses such drugs beyond the recommended prescription, it is already categorized as an addiction.

Some of the commonly abused drugs are Opioids, Xanax, Ativan, Valium, Klonopin, Adderall, Concerta, Daytrana, Methylin, and Ritalin. These are painkillers, stimulants, or depressants and should only be taken in the amount and frequency advised by a physician.

Many aren't aware of it, but these drugs are powerful enough to affect the brain's functions and processes. This, in turn, makes it necessary to avoid overuse. Otherwise, a person will experience the same mental long-term effects of illegal drugs. This is also why doctors are careful not to prescribe too much of one medicine. Many popular figures have reportedly died from overdose of prescription drugs; two notable personalities are actor Heath Ledger and singer Michael Jackson.

Addiction is never limited to substance abuse. Instead of drowning oneself in mind- and body-altering products, a person can repeatedly reward himself compulsively through acts and behaviors despite the presence of consequences it has on relationships, finances, and one's personal life. These are what experts refer to as *behavioral addiction*, and these are:

1. *Sex*

   Who doesn't love sex? According to Sigmund Freud, everything a person does and every decision he makes is primarily driven by the need to mate. When it is done in incredulous frequency, however, it may already fall within the bounds of addiction.

   Understand that compulsively masturbating to pornography or opting for computer and phone sex services does not necessarily make a person an addict. Yes, it could mark the beginning, but most people with this behavioral problem do not *merely* seek the pleasure of orgasm. Some actually stretch the limits of the experience by participating in taboo sexual acts like exhibitionism, voyeurism, and other consensual quirks and fetishes. And several others extend beyond the walls of ethics and law by making obscene phone calls, molesting a minor, or rape.

It is difficult to say, however, if an individual has sexual addiction or not because sex is more often a manifestation or a result of stress, depression, and even anger.

2. *Internet*
Although there are no instant physically damaging effects of being online the entire day, it has the capacity to destroy a person's sense of reality and end relationships with actual friends and family members.

With the increasing proliferation of mobile phones and other portable electronic gadgets, however, it has become almost impossible to differentiate a typical social media whore (as commonly termed by netizens or avid internet users) from an actual internet addict. To give a clearer picture, one good example of this kind of addiction is the people who engage in virtual reality games, like The Sims. Mere participation is harmless, of course, but there are those who invest extensive time, money, and effort in living inside these make-believe communities more than they do in reality. These people create the ideal versions of themselves in these pixelated worlds then build relationships with other virtual characters controlled by random strangers elsewhere across the globe. Some even go as far as entering marriage with their virtual lovers despite not having met the person behind it.

There are, of course, less severe manifestations of this addiction. Although they do this uncontrollably, some settle with surfing the internet for topics of interest, socializing, and participating in public chats and forums, and minute by minute updates of the person's thoughts, feelings, and activities.

3. *Food*

   Food addiction has been added to the list only recently because it's only now that scientists have begun to understand that obesity is not really lack of control, but an effect of unhealthy food on the body.

   Basically, this is actually less of a behavioral and more of a consumption problem. Just like drugs and nicotine, most processed foods contain ingredients that shoot massive amounts of dopamine. Sugary foods can also trigger this addiction because high amounts of such foods disrupt the hormonal balance of the body. This imbalance consequently prevents the brain from recognizing the hormones that signal fullness, and instead, see those that signal hunger. This is the reason why despite having recently eaten, a person remains hungry.

4. *Gambling*

   Some experts also refer to this as compulsive gambling. Although illegal in some if not most territories of the world, it is logically harmless. It is normal for a person to experience a specific kind of "high" when winning like in any other activity that gives a sense of achievement from luck. Gambling becomes an addiction when life, work, family, or friends start to get affected one way or another.

   Basically, a person with this kind of addiction cannot think of anything but gambling. It doesn't matter as well if they are up or down, happy or depressed, or broke or well-off. It's all they could think of and all they want to do, even if the odds are against them. Understand as well that even if a person can afford to lose thousands or even millions of dollars, it remains a problem if relationships and friendships break down because of it.

   Another important thing to note about gambling addiction is that a person does not have to do it every day to be considered an addict. He only becomes so when, despite his full awareness of the consequences, he still pursues the habit.

5. *Video games*
This is another supposedly harmless invention of mankind that had somehow evolved into another form of addiction. Understand, however, that not all gamers are addicts, like how frustrated and angry parents accuse their children of being. It is normal for gamers to feel irritated and annoyed when being pulled from the game because these require full attention and concentration. The time that parents and guardians should begin to worry is when these gamers become restless, moody, and depressed when not playing. In some extreme cases of video game addiction, players would often, if not completely, overlook their basic needs such as eating, sleeping, and even excreting.

Some experts pointed out that a probable cause of video game addiction is the sense of achievement and fulfillment it imparts.

6. *Work*
Since being a workaholic is something worth praising in modern society, it is often overlooked as a psychological problem. It is, however, a prevailing problem, and more people are falling into this demise unchecked every year because society itself is pushing them to it. The common roots of work addiction after all are ambition (the need to succeed and achieve a higher status in life) and escapism (the need to draw one's attention from emotional stress).

Being highly productive isn't bad, but everything done in excess is. Working to the point that the person is unable to establish and even maintain stable relationships with friends and family makes it an addiction. Those who regularly sacrifice Friday nights out with friends to burn extra hours in the office can already be considered addicts. Some would even refrain from going on vacations because they are under the illusion that work needs them more.

7. *Shopping*
This is one addiction many women are familiar with. Either they are admittedly shopping addicts themselves or they are fans of Sophie Kinsella's *Confessions of a Shopaholic* novel. Despite being a work of fiction, it perfectly describes what shopping addiction is. It is basically a compulsion to purchase things out of impulse rather than need. Much like how it is with workaholism, shopping addiction is observed as a way for most to escape their emotions.

There are studies, however, showing a physical response to the act of buying that leads to addiction. Some scientists noted the release of endorphins and dopamine in the brain when a person shops. And as explained previously, these hormones are responsible for giving that "high" feeling to which psychologically unstable people are prone to getting addicted.

8. *Plastic surgery*
Not many people can afford plastic surgery, but there are individuals who find themselves craving for more after having gone under the knife once. This is typically fueled by their desire to transform into the obscured definition of beauty dictated by society. In other words, it is a way for people to overcome their endless physical insecurities. And in some cases, people develop an obsession to looking like their favorite icon. A few examples of this are the real life Barbie and Ken, and a boy who paid a hundred thousand dollars to simply look like Justin Bieber.

The result of these desires is an endless need to look "perfect." Because of that, plastic surgery addicts are willing to pay for these procedures and go under the knife countless times just to appease themselves mentally and emotionally. What makes this case worse is the lack of laws restricting the number of times a person can opt for plastic surgery for aesthetic reasons.

There is also what's called BDD or Body Dysmorphic Disorder. People who have this psychological problem see themselves as ugly despite looking attractive to other people. There are some Hollywood beauties who had this, and they all ended ruining their exceptional faces by going through plastic surgery. People who have this mental condition do not necessarily become surgery addicts, but they are prone to it.

Although rare, it is not impossible for two addictions, one from each category, to be adopted by a person. For instance, an individual can be a drug addict and a sex addict at the same time. When this happens, however, self-help may no longer be enough to curb the addictions.

The True Fuels of Addiction

Psychological problems do not simply appear on a person. These could be rooted deep in their past – a traumatic experience, a history of abuse, or an unforgettable emotionally scarring incident. In some cases, it's simply the fact that people are morally flawed, or that they lack education on society and ethics. The addictions these types of individuals harbor, however, usually involve drugs and other substances.

Addiction is, in reality, a psychological problem. While some addicts are aware of the harm that their behavior does to them and the people around them, some do not have the knowledge of how serious the circumstances they are in are. Some are even completely unaware that they are addicted to a particular activity, which makes them fail to recognize that they need help.

For this reason, addiction is defined as the compulsion to engage in particular activities or to use a substance, without regard to potential consequences that can be devastating to an addict's well-being.

Experts also accept that there is a clear relationship between addiction and mental illness. For most people who are helping others deal with addiction, they claim that addiction is a mental disorder because it involves abuse. At the same time, it is assumed that many addicts have psychiatric issues such as psychoses, anxiety and self-esteem issues, post-traumatic syndrome disorders, and several other personality disorders. For that reason, it is important for people to understand that apart from getting over any physical impacts of their addictions, they have to recover mentally and emotionally as well.

Addiction is All About Control

If you feel that you are addicted to any substance, activity, object, or a person, you need to understand that you may have a problem when it comes to control. You feel that you are only in control of how you feel and decide whenever you have the opportunity to have the very thing that you are addicted to, and then you feel that you are lost without it. You may think that you have the ability to judge what you can or cannot do, when the matter of fact is, you are being controlled by the very thing that you are addicted to.

When you experience addiction, you are experiencing dependency, which deprives you of the knowledge of what truly is happening around you. That, in turn, leads to denial of the real problems that you are facing, and the problems that your addiction has created. If you think that the substance, activity, object, or person that you are addicted to is the only thing that can give you pleasure, you are denying yourself the ability to make better choices when it comes to being happy. You are also making the world smaller, and your life bleak and solitary.

Self control is, of course, applicable only in addictions without physiologically altering capabilities; examples of such addictions are gambling, work, shopping, and sex. There are dependencies, however, that, despite the person's desire to change, cannot be easily controlled because these had already impaired logic and reason. Apart from substance abuse, one behavioral addiction that causes changes in the hormones and brain function is food addiction. In these cases, telling yourself or a friend in need to *take control* wouldn't help a lot because the substance had already literally and physiologically taken control.

When that happens, the first thing you need to do is accept the truth. Acknowledge the fact that you are an addict, and more importantly, embrace the need to change and stop. Willpower still has a lot to do with this, but it alone will not suffice. And this is where seeking the help and support of both friends and family will come (More of this will be discussed in the later chapters.).

Why is It Wrong When It is Pleasurable?

When you look at the things that people can become addicted to, you would see that somewhat they are designed to provide pleasure to a person, or that it can be a very normal activity, such as shopping, eating and exercising. At this point, better think that the things that can be addicting are not all illegal. A person can become compulsive about certain normal things such as buying shoes, and when it becomes excessive, it becomes a serious problem.

Before proceeding further, it is important for you to know the process going on in the brain to understand why even the simple act of buying a pair of shoes can lead to addiction. Basically, as explained previously, it all begins with dopamine. As discussed, this chemical in the brain is the body's very own stock of happiness. In fact, it is the tangible form of happiness itself because without it, a person will most likely never see the silver lining of every dark, brooding cloud.

Now, when a person eats, drinks, works, has sex, or even makes a purchase, dopamine is secreted by the brain. This, in turn, will give the person a sense of pleasure in the activity. And since pleasure is directly related to reward, the person's consciousness will develop an understanding that the activity or substance must be repeated.

Of course, there are a lot of things in life that can give this feeling. Furthermore, eating, for example, is the very foundation of human survival, as well as sex. The reason why the brain would find pleasure in it, and would want to repeat it is because the body needs it. So then, how can it become a form of obsession or dependency?

The answer is how fast dopamine travels to the brain. In other words, the faster this chemical reaches the brain, the more pleasurable the experience is, and illegal drugs happen to know the shortcut.

This is, of course, coupled by another natural process in the brain called tolerance. Imagine it as the human body's version of engine brakes. Orgasm, for example, is the best feeling in the world when you first experienced it. Now, the reason why you seek to have sex again is to experience that same feeling, and that is very normal. The problem comes, however, when the act is repeated over and over in the same manner. It gets boring. The same explosion of pleasure you experienced the first time you tried it just isn't there anymore, and this is because of tolerance. Basically, the brain lowers the amount of dopamine it secretes when experiencing the same acts.

Naturally, the result of this would be loss of interest, or moderated involvement or consumption, in the act or substance. However, the memory of that same wonderful feeling persists. And as mentioned before, if a person has mental instability, he is prone to developing a compulsion or a motivation to experience it again from the same stimulant. From the example above, for instance, if normal sex isn't pleasurable anymore, the person will be driven to seek something more exciting and thrilling, like BDSM or orgies. And basically, this is how the habit becomes an addiction from then on. This is also why, in some instances, the act has evolved into extreme or severe cases that are dangerous not only to the person, but to the people around him as well.

Anyone wanting to cure themselves of addiction – or those who seek to help a friend – should understand the enemy before anything else. You need to have a better grasp of what's happening in your body and how addiction can come in varied forms. Doing so will help you fight it and give you enough willpower to overcome it.

Chapter 2: Are You an Addict?

No one in their right mind intentionally wanted to become an addict. Every addiction started as an innocent first try (except perhaps in the case of trying illegal drugs, unless driven by peer pressure), or a way to address a need. But somehow, somewhere along the road, something wrong happened and the person unknowingly fell into this trap. The worst part of this, however, is that an individual willingly submits to it.

Because of that, with the impairment of logic and reason, it is almost impossible for a person to recognize the fact that he has a problem. Reading through this, however, makes you an exception.

When you picked up this book, you probably:

1. Have some problem dealing with any compulsive behavior and you are acknowledging that it has become difficult for you to live a normal life, or

2. You have a loved one or a friend that has been experiencing problems with compulsions.

With this book, you would be able to understand when to actually start looking for symptoms. You'll also learn how to tell whether you are having a real problem.

Now, the first thing that you need to do is to identify whether you are dealing with a problem with addiction.

Signs and Symptoms of Addiction

You may be dealing with an addiction problem if you are experiencing the following:

1. You have an activity that you cannot stop. You may have attempted to stop doing it, but it was unsuccessful.

2. You feel that when you have an attempt to stop an activity, you develop physical and mood-related symptoms. You feel that the only way to make sure that you're happy is to continuously do it.

2. You sacrifice other activities in order to make sure that you are able to continuously perform the activity that you are addicted to. In your mind, it is the only thing worth doing.

3. You make sure that you have adequate resources to make sure that you are able to do the activity. You may tend to have numerous credit cards or have a separate savings account to make sure that you would be able to freely do that particular activity. At the same time, you make sure that these resources are unknown to anyone.

4. You have financial difficulties because of the activity that you are addicted to. You tend to borrow money or sell belongings in order to make sure that you would be able to do it.

5. Your relationships begin to suffer because of the activity that you are addicted to. You tend to be involved in fights whenever someone bothers you or tries to stop you from doing that particular activity. At the same time, you feel that it is okay to pay less attention to how they feel or spend less time with other people, as long as you would be able to do what you want to do.

6. When you are confronted by other people about your activity, you deny or refuse to acknowledge that you have a problem. At the same time, you believe that your compulsions may be the only things that help you feel calm or satisfied.

7. You are beginning to fear authorities or you have problems with the law.

8. You feel that because you continuously do an activity, you are living in solitude and you do that activity in secrecy.

9. You begin to have secret stashes. You also feel that you have to have immediate access to that activity that you cannot stop doing. For example, if you cannot stop smoking, you hide packs of cigarettes at the back of your medicine cabinet or even in your vault.

10. You feel that you are obligated to drop other recreations or hobbies because you cannot sustain them anymore. At the same time you also feel that your money should be spent mostly on the activity that you feel that you need to do.

11. You begin to take risks in order to ensure that you continue to do that particular activity. You feel that nothing can stop you when it comes to doing what you want.

Addiction is a serious problem because it interferes with the things that you need to do in order to survive and have a healthy life. For this reason, it is necessary that you address this problem right away.

Know, however, that not all of the above enumerated symptoms need to be checked to consider yourself or a friend an addict. It is a case to case basis since not all addictions are against the law, like working, shopping, and eating – unless the person begins borrowing money. One's observation should be focused on the person's behavior because this provides the most concrete evidence of addiction.

And the best way to make behavioral symptoms such as irritation, moodiness, and temper manifest is by depriving yourself or a friend of the act or substance of addiction. Withdraw him from the activity and watch carefully how he would behave in such situations.

Why Did You Have this Problem?

There are many reasons why people have resorted to abusing substances or to compulsively do an activity. And the reason encompasses the chemical design of the brain, as well as the presence of psychological instability.

The scientific explanation as discussed in the previous chapter is but a presentation of what happens in you chemically to make sense of it. And as explained previously, psychological instability isn't unconsciously adopted without cause.

Humans are sentient beings and, no matter how shallow, there has to be a conscious or unconscious motivation or driving force to make them submit to addiction. And this is where the many possible reasons come in, making it almost impossible to provide a single and linear solution to dependency.

1. Personal Factors
    It is clear that your addiction may actually have been caused by other issues that you may have not addressed in the past, and you are relying on your addiction to make you feel relaxed, happy, or in control.

    For a lot of addicts, they think that performing activities that soon led to addiction was their ticket to acceptance. Others think that they can only deal with anxiety if they abuse food, alcohol, tobacco, or drugs. Some think that they will have a better appearance if they throw the food that they eat out or exercise too much. Some feel that if they gamble or play too many video games, they will have a sense of achievement.

2. External Factors
    Of course, there are possibly more severe causes or past experiences that could drive a person to addiction, and these go beyond personal needs such as

belongingness or acceptance. These are causes brought upon by external factors, perhaps by the people around them or the nature of the environment they grew up in.

A neglected child is a good example here. The external factor would be the parents for they had the responsibility over the minor. Whether the neglect was intentional or not, it will negatively impact the child. This will not necessarily result in a rebellious attitude, of course, or a rowdy and uncontrollable character, but it will surely affect the way the child views love, trust, and affection.

As he grows up, he will carry these perspectives and behave according to them. It is likely for him to develop internet addiction, for instance, and seek attention and at the same time impart much caring and devotion to the people he had never seen before. In Maslow's hierarchy of needs, love and belongingness sit at the middle of the pyramid. Therefore, it is only natural for people to seek and express love. From this example, however, it is the manner and idea of giving affection that was impaired.

Of course, included here are the more horrific causes such as rape, molestation, kidnapping, and torture. If these experiences aren't expressed and treated, and if the person isn't given ample proper support by friends and family, then it will surely evolve into an addiction.

What is the common factor that ties up all addicts? They feel that they are lost without the compulsive behavior, and the world that they have created with their dependency on their activities would crumble. However, when you look at it, things could be a lot better without addiction. Addiction ultimately makes you lose your grasp on reality and look away from the real problems. Instead of allowing you to think of the right remedy for real life problems, addiction covers them up and over time, provides more problems that you can handle.

Now, how can you get started to live without addiction? The next chapter will tell you about the first thing that you need to do.

Chapter 3: Debunking the Myth about Recovery

Some people think that addicts need to hit rock bottom in order for them to be aware that they have been doing something wrong. However, it does not apply to everyone. You have to understand that there are some people that actually do not realize that they have been doing something that could possibly harm them in the long run. They may not even realize that the root cause of their current problems is their addiction, and then they blame their problems to something else.

Common Misconceptions of Addiction and Recovery

The first step towards recovery is learning the misconceptions of addiction because these could be the very reason why an addict is in constant denial of their condition. There is, after all, a well-formed stigma associated with the matter. Society has, in turn, responded to this matter in such a discriminating way that addicts draw greater comfort from continuing their habits instead of seeking help.

1. *Becoming an addict is a choice.*
   As discussed in the previous chapter in both scientific and psychological aspects, being an addict is not a choice. Several personally damaging traps and snares are scattered all throughout life, and these people just happen to fall on addiction.

   The important thing to note in this myth is to throw away the prejudices you harbored from society's and the media's wrongful representations of addiction. Society sees these people as either weak-willed or inherently bad or immoral, and that is the worst way to view these people. Apparently, it is this very discrimination that prevents them from coming clean. People with a lack of understanding fail to comprehend that addicts want to recover from the habit as much as a cancer-stricken patient would want to heal from his condition. And it is this lack of understanding from their own kind that pushes them further into the habit.

Furthermore, addiction does not automatically make them a bad person, which is usually how movies and television portray them to be. They are just like you in the sense that they just want to get through each day. It's just that they can't do it without the activity or substance to which they are addicted. They don't want to rob your house, or smash you in the head with a baseball bat to steal your wallet, or kidnap your child.

2. *A person with addiction is easy to differentiate.*
    Try to imagine what an addict looks like. For sure, the general image that appeared in your head was a person in dirty ragged clothes, living in isolation, with no friends or family, has no job (or if he has, it's a blue collar job like scrubbing toilets or washing dishes), and goes home to a rundown shack in a shabby part of town. Although these traits are true in some instances, the vast majority of addicts actually looks like you – and may even be better off financially.

These people function normally in society. They have jobs, may even have families, and may also have a deep devotion to a religion. Understand, however, that most of the time, addicts use, and even showcase, these factors to hide their habit, and it's all because of the stigma explained in the previous number. This image, however, does not mean he can afford his addiction. Some friends and family had to wait for the addict to reach rock-bottom before they extend a helping hand, or before they even realize the person is an addict. This is what everyone should avoid; waiting for the last and almost irreversible moment before acting on it. If the signs are present in the person despite the showcasing of wealth and stability, conduct an intervention. Never wait for him to become the image of addiction initially described.

3. *Genetics play a role in addiction.*
    People believe the road to dependency is paved by their ancestors. It is said that if an uncle, your mother, or even your brother had been an addict, you are prone to becoming one yourself. Although there are facts supporting this, it's not always the case. As explained before, the person's environment and personal experiences will greatly contribute to the development of addiction. In other words, the root cause of dependency isn't a single factor, but complicated interwoven fibers of nurture and nature. It's a different case for everyone. Therefore, if a form of intervention or recovery worked on one individual, it does not assure that it will work on another.

    Additionally, just because you have become an addict and you discovered that someone else in the family had been one, never think recovery is futile. Thinking this and giving in lead to the opposite road of self salvation. At the same time, if the family record is clean of addiction, this does not mean you are safe from becoming one. Never have the confidence to try illegal substances thinking you have natural resistance to addiction.

4. *Addicts are damaged before and even after recovery.*
    It is true that taking harmful substances can rewire the brain. As explained earlier, it has the capacity to alter chemical and hormonal secretions and thus impair logic and reason. This, however, does not transform one into a useless zombie permanently. As explained before, these people can function normally in society. And should they even reach a point in their addiction where they seem to have completely

succumbed to the substance, there remains a piece of consciousness that holds on to the will to change and recover. Otherwise, how could some even find their way back to sobriety and complete recovery? Therefore, it is wrong to think of them as damaged people, because they are not. They have simply lost their way.

Another problem for most rehabilitated addicts is how difficult it is for them to find a job after immersing back in society. Employers believe they are damaged goods, and that the only thing these people are capable of is waiting for their expiration to arrive. This is completely untrue. Once an addict is out of the habit, his brain functions return to normal (although genetics and addiction history will play a role in the whole recovery process). If they want to, they can study for an MBA, become a doctor, or engage in business and succeed. However, because of the continuing image that addiction can permanently destroy a person's functionality, they are being deprived of opportunities to get their lives back.

This is another reason why those who stumbled upon dependency decide to keep the habit a secret. There is no hope to get their lives back because even if they recover and stay sober, society will scrutinize the giant crack addiction embedded in their lives. Therefore, if you want to help others, and even yourself, this false idea should be corrected.

What is Recovery Exactly?

If you are suffering from addiction and you want to recover from it, you may need to see that it is better to jump from the boat than to sink with it. When you say that you are "in recovery", it doesn't mean that you are simply trying to stop abusing a substance or a compulsive behavior. It means that you are aiming to embrace massive change. According to the Substance Abuse and Mental Health Services Administration

(SAMHSA), recovery is the course where a person undergoes change through which he is able to abstain from his compulsion and achieves improved quality of life, wellness, and health.

The Twelve Guiding Principles of Recovery

When you choose to define your recovery, you need to understand that there are guiding pillars that would help you understand that this is the best thing that you can do for yourself. The following principles would help you fully understand why choosing recovery is the best decision:

1. There are several different pathways to recovery, which means that there is no one way to stop an addiction.

2. Your recovery is empowering and is self-directed.

3. Your recovery means that it should involve the recognition that you need transformation and change.

4. Your recovery is always holistic.

5. Your recovery is something that your loved ones and friends support.

6. Your recovery is also partly the process of healing yourself and redefining your life.

7. Your recovery also means that you are joining or rejoining your community, and you are building or rebuilding your life with it.

8. Your recovery springs from the idea that you have hope, and that you are thankful for the life and the support given to you.

9. Your recovery addresses all the problems that people have when it comes to discrimination. You transcend stigma and shame when you get past your addiction. It is also supported by dealing with and addressing trauma.

10. Your recovery involves societal and cultural dimensions. It does not exist in a vacuum.

11. Your recovery means improving your health and promoting wellness.

12. Your recovery is part of reality. It has happened to someone else. It can and will happen to you.

When you look at the very thing that you are trying to achieve, you are making a commitment to make sure that you improve yourself, and then contribute more to society by ensuring that you are a more responsible citizen. You also see to it that the next years of your life is directed towards improvement.

You can only start improving when you know that you can troubleshoot your life and identify what your problem really is. The next chapter will tell you what you need to do in order to start identifying what your goals should be.

Chapter 4: The First Steps to Recovery

Now that you know more about addiction – what it does to the brain, how it starts, and how the habit worsens – it's time to learn the first courses of action to recovery. Just like in the case of a baby learning to walk, the first few steps are the hardest but are nonetheless the most crucial ones.

Should there be any confusion along the way, or if you forgot the reason why you should opt for this, always look back at the previous chapter's **12 Guiding Principles to Recovery.** Essentially, this will help in pushing you or your friend to regain that good life that everyone deserves.

As mentioned earlier, not one single form of treatment is applicable to every addict. It is a case to case basis. Therefore, it is important to assess everything about the person first.

I. Seek Support

You may want to seek the help of a trusted friend or family member in recovering from addiction. Much like with depression, recovering from addiction requires support, and it is best to find one from the moment you accept your addiction. It may be too much to ask for, but this person should accompany you through the whole process – from beginning to end. This is necessary because most of the addicts who want to seek professional help often change their minds even before stepping into their office. With someone there to push your back, chances of recovering from dependency are higher.

There are, of course, hesitations and pitfalls when looking at people for support, and these are some of the ways to overcome them as well as other available options for finding support:

- Family and friends may not always be your first choice. Why? Because it is inevitable that somewhere along the way, you have caused them great trouble, you're currently in a fight with them, or that the relationship has already ended. Luckily, there are such things as family therapy and couples counseling available throughout the country. These programs involve families or friends during therapy sessions to basically allow professionals explain to them why you need support. This is so you won't have to face all by yourself the people to whom you owe so much, and that they attain a better understanding of your situation.

- Friends may not also be the best option for support, especially if they were the ones who introduced you to the habit in the first place or if they are addicts themselves. Therefore, it is necessary that you build a new social network, and a sober one. Finding the right people to understand your situation, however, may be difficult. As explained earlier, the stigma that revolves around addiction remains strong. In this case, joining a neighborhood tea party or book club may not present the most supportive people. What you need are those who have seen the worst of society and still extend a helping hand. Thus, your best options are joining church or civic groups, volunteer programs (Be a volunteer and not the type of person that these programs aim to help.), or art classes (People with addiction often keep their negative emotions compressed inside their chest. Through art, they can express these and temporarily relieve any driving force to succumb to their habit. Members of such classes aren't as keen on discriminating addicts as well because their perspectives on life aren't contained in a structured and black and white way.).

- If it's the environment (the house and even the neighborhood) itself that's not conducive to recovery, then it's time to move to a new home. This is where moving to a rehab or sober living home may become necessary. If the ones near you require a certain amount of money to get in, then you may need to find other options. What's important here is for you to live in a drug-free environment. Consider finding a home through relatives living in good neighborhoods or by inquiring in churches if they run salvation homes.

- Support groups are always the best option. Find one with meetings held in a place near you, and make it a point to attend every meeting. If you prefer people who can completely empathize with you, then there is no better option because they are fighting the same battle as you. Of course, choose a support group that directly addresses your addiction. If you are, for example, a sex addict, then look for a sex addiction support group and not just a generic "addiction support group."

You don't have to exclusively choose one from the listed options above. If you can find all of these then go forth and approach them. Recovery, as already mentioned, is a complete turnaround of one's life, and this is difficult even for normal people. Therefore, it is essential that you get the most support you can.

II. How to Assess Yourself

So far, you have identified that you have a problem, and that is addiction. At this point, it is time for you to talk it out and seek the necessary measures. The best way to do this is to talk about your concerns with an expert when it comes to rehabilitation.

Remember to keep a friend or your family, or anyone who supports your recovery, close to you in this process. They need to know what the result of this assessment will be so they are duly informed of everything. Understand that they are as responsible to your recovery as you – this is the kind of support you will need – so whenever something needs to be done or exercised, they are there to remind you, push you, and keep you motivated.

The government and private organizations offer a lot of channels when it comes to addressing any kind of addiction. When you make it to an assessment meeting, make sure that you do the following:

1. Say the truth.

If you are aware that you are suffering from any type of addiction and you are in an assessment meeting, see to it that you tell professionals about all the symptoms that you are experiencing. Do not downplay any information and do not be afraid – these organizations protect your rights and they make sure that everything that you share would remain confidential.

2. Tell them about your concerns.

If you feel that you are in deep trouble or that your family and other relationships may be suffering because of your addiction, tell them about it. Your concerns would always be relevant, and that would point to the completeness and accuracy of your diagnosis. At the same time, make sure that you also tell them any concerns about their process, if there is any.

3. Recognize your emotions.

Expect that questionnaires and other procedures would make you feel several emotions regarding your addiction. However, those procedures are actually intended to make you become aware of what you really think of your compulsion.

4. Realize your support system.

When you are moving towards recovery, understand that you are not doing this alone. While it is imperative to talk to a professional, it is also important to communicate with your loved ones.

Being able to go through this process would enable you to understand that you are enabled and empowered to change. The next chapter would explain the preliminary things that you need to do to make your efforts to recover count.

Chapter 5: Making the Commitment to Recover

Now that you are aware that you have all the help that you need in order for you to make your way to recovery, it's time to actually make it happen. The following should serve as your goals from now on:

1. Make your recovery your number one goal.

Think about yourself – that compulsive behavior is in no way stronger than you. Drugs and alcohol consumption, gambling, or shopping does not happen without your consent. You are the one that is in control of your actions. At the same time, making that commitment that you would stick to recovering from addiction makes you more empowered about your choices.

Note that your primary goal is not to minimize, but to avoid that particular compulsive behavior altogether. Starting today, it is your obligation to stay away from any temptation that would rear you back to your problematic behavior. If you have been abusing alcohol and tobacco, clean your house and remove anything that relates to them. If you are addicted to shopping, cut all your credit cards and make a list of all the things that you only need to buy.

2. Understand that recovery takes one step at a time.

Your addiction does not go away overnight and you have to see that recovery is a lengthy process. However, each day you live with the commitment to recovery makes you a much better person.

3. Have a healthy regimen.

If you want to feel clean, then you need to live clean. Make sure that starting today, you are going to commit to having a healthy diet and physical regimen. Clean your house and get rid of all your stashes – you are not going to need them anymore. Get complete rest and eat healthy. Make sure that you are complementing that healthy diet with ample exercise. You would feel more energetic and positive about life.

4. Have a healthy hobby.

If you are doing something worth your time, you would think less about the compulsion that you want to get over with. If you have a particular schedule that you used to keep to make way for your addiction, replace it with a healthy recreation. If you are spending Thursday nights for binge drinking, make sure that you use that time instead to help in a charity or take lessons. Not only will these activities help you have new friends and new experiences, they will also help you develop self-esteem and achieve a sense of accomplishment.

5. Join a support group.

This was already mentioned earlier, and it will be mentioned again. Understand that this is the most important part of recovery and that it will play a significant role even after you have succeeded. This road, after all, is best traveled with a companion.

While you have your friends and family to support you, recovery would be a lot easier if you are also surrounded by other people who are going through the same thing. It'll also be advantageous to seek professional and spiritual help. Go around the community to find a group that you could belong to. Not only would you hear about a lot of success stories, you would also have easy access to all the help that you need when it comes to recovery.

6. Never give up.

Recovery is a possibility and a reality as long as you stay committed to it. Your obligation to yourself and your community is stronger than your addiction.

When you think about all the things that you need to do in order to make sure that you are on the right path, you'll be encouraged to live a clean slate, and immediately see the future wherein you are living a holistic and healthy life. Being able to see that future would always give you that hope that the challenges that you're facing would soon be over and that you would live a free life.

Chapter 6: The Bumpy Road to Recovery

As you may notice, all throughout this book, several mind setting reminders are enumerated. That's because addiction recovery is more of a mental endeavor than a physical one. It will revolve around control, and despite the support you are encouraged to get from loved ones, most of the work will still fall on your shoulders. In other words, you are accountable to what this recovery will lead to.

That sounded all too intimidating, and it truly is, but that's why you have this book to help you. Basically, the guides and reminders enumerated below will help you get through the hardest of times—when the temptation to succumb to the habit is at its strongest.

Battling with Urges

Sometimes, it's easy to think of committing to something. When the urge is there, however, the voices that had kept you motivated to recover will drown against the call of the habit. Never lose hope when this happens. It does not mean you are being weak-willed or that the treatment isn't going well. These urges are normal, and you will encounter them more often than you did before.

Keep in mind that changes in one's daily habits will only make something more irresistible. Weight loss, for instance, requires that a person remove any kind of sugary foods from their diet. The challenge will be easy enough during the first few days, or even hours, but the longer the absence of cake is, the more irresistible the sight of cake becomes. The same concept applies to addiction.

Now you may not know this yet, but these urges are often triggered by certain emotions or specific events. The reason why you began the habit, after all, is to dampen unwanted emotions (whether it is loneliness, anger, frustration, shame, anxiety, or hopelessness) or to escape problems. Understand, however, that these forms of emotional and mental stresses will remain despite your dedication to getting your life back on track.

Fortunately, there are ways on how to cope with urges, and that's by making changes in how you address stress. There are several different ways, and all of them will be enumerated below. Your job now is to check which one will work best for you.

- *Exercise.* There are several reasons why people exercise, and one of them is to relieve anger. This is what prevents most CEOs and general managers from hitting people in the face. They wear their boxing gloves and turn to their punching bags then give it all they've got. Don't think, however, that this is just some way to relieve primal urges. Scientifically speaking, when the body engages in exercise, endorphins are released. And as explained in the first chapter, this is a hormone that contributes to the feeling of happiness or pleasure. Therefore, whenever you feel stressed or emotionally compromised, try running or walking around in a nice park, or engage in any physical activity you enjoy.

- *Enjoy beautiful landscapes.* And this means you have to go outside your house, savor the fresh clean air, and feel the warm sun. This, of course, is good if your home is close to nature, like in the beach or the woods. Otherwise, schedule a last-minute nature trip in a nearby park or mountain, river or lake, beach or island, after a hard day at work and just enjoy life's natural gifts.

- *Yoga or meditation.* These two disciplines are specifically centered on finding inner peace. And if you've watched the animated film *Kung Fu Panda 2*, you'd know that inner peace is the answer to completely eliminating any kind of stress or worries in one's life. This, of course, requires continuous work, so don't get frustrated when inner peace doesn't come to you immediately. What's important when you engage in these activities is that you are progressively stepping away from the habit.

- *Adopt a pet.* Studies have proven that brushing your hands against a pet's fur can lower your stress levels. Therefore, every time you feel stressed or sad, look for the comfort of a cat or a dog and let them make you feel loved. This, of course, does not mean you have to go and adopt a furry friend, especially if you don't have the capacity to place an animal under your responsibility. You can always befriend a neighbor with a dog and visit him and his pet whenever you feel the urge. A little chat, coffee, and play time is, after all, a great way to relax. Another option is for you to visit cat cafes or dog cafes. These have become popular quite recently, and you are assured that the animals here are well-groomed and adorably friendly.

- *Listen to calming music.* This is probably the fastest way to change one's mood, or at least make one more relaxed. These melodies, however, are those with smooth flowing tunes like with orchestras, piano performances, and music box lullabies. Songs with lyrics are good, but be selective with what you include in your "relaxation" playlist. You don't want to trigger unwanted memories or feelings or to fan your emotions the wrong way.

- *Seek beautiful scents and smells.* It is a scientifically proven fact that smell is directly connected to memory, explaining why the whiff of a scent can make you recall long forgotten memories. So if you have a beautiful memory you can associate with a scent, then breathe it in. A good example of this could be that wonderful date with your spouse in a coffee shop. Inhale the smell of coffee beans to relish the memory and keep your mind away from your addiction.

Smell doesn't have to be exclusively used for this purpose. You can also try keeping scented candles close by. The fragrances and essences locked in these wax cylinders are designed to help you relax. So whenever you feel the world is against you, light up a candle and let its scent fill the room as well as your soul.

- *Reward yourself with a hot bath.* This is the best complement of scented candles. Warm water is proven to help wash away worries and anxieties. Religiously soaking in a hot bath after a long day at work can help you make notable progress in your battle against addiction.

- *Browse through old family photos.* Whenever you clean the house and you stumble upon an old photo album, you always get that urge to sit and look at all the beautiful memories that had gone by – the days when you were still young and innocent. Not only is this a good way to escape from house cleaning, it can also take your mind away from the urge to submit to your habit.

- *Massage.* Give yourself a massage or get one in a nearby spa. The quickest way to eliminate stress is by targeting your head and shoulders. So if you are in the middle of travel, or work, or any important activity, give yourself a quick massage in these areas. But if your time allows it, get a full-body massage from a certified therapist. One hour of it is said to be equivalent to a full eight hours of sleep.

What you want to aim for is to make one or two of these a complete habit. It's like in fighting the urge to smoke. Those who try to quit keep a steady supply of candy or gum in their pockets so that when they feel the need to light a stick, they just chew on one of these sweets. The same concept should be adopted during recovery. It can easily help the brain rewire from the addiction to this new and harmless habit. Think of it as learning and practice. If you don't stick to one of these, your brain would scramble to think of what to do every time your urge kicks in. With the new habit readily available in your pocket, house, or workplace, all you'd need to do next is reach out.

Staying Away from Pitfalls and Triggers

If there are good habits to adopt, there are also pitfalls to avoid. Dealing with stress is one thing, but even when you are having a great time or following doctor's orders, the dangers of falling back into the habit is just one bad decision away. Below are some places and situations you should avoid and observe to maintain progress in your recovery.

1. *Temporarily sever your ties with your addict friends.* This means if you're a shopaholic, try not to join your girlfriends for a while even if you'll just have coffee. If in case you are a workaholic, try to make friends in the office and choose those who habitually go on nature trips or vacations then let them drag you along. Basically, stay away from anyone who might endanger your progress. If they are your real friends, they will understand. However, if they don't support your cause, then it's time to completely burn the bridge.

2. *Avoid drinking, clubbing, or visiting any establishment overflowing with alcohol.* You may not be a substance abuser, but the fact that you are distancing from your behavioral addiction makes you vulnerable to alcoholism. The mentally blurring effects of alcohol make it easier for you to fight urges, and this is not particularly the ideal habit to substitute your old one.

3. *Be open to medical professionals about your history of substance abuse.* This generally applies when you

are having your dentals checked, or other instances where a physician may have to prescribe you with medicine. The reason why this is important is so they could avoid prescribing you with highly potent drugs that could lead you to relapse. Never feel shameful or humiliated when opening up about these things, especially to a medical professional. They are trained to handle sensitive personal information, after all.

4. *Exercise caution when taking prescription drugs.* Also included in the list of addictive substances are prescription drugs. Therefore, if you have been under sleeping pills, painkillers, or anti-anxiety medication, it's best if you stay away from them for a while or exercise caution in using them while in recovery. Just like with alcohol, you don't want these to become your new habit because somehow, you are still vulnerable.

Surviving Powerful Cravings

There is a difference between cravings and urges. When compared to weight loss, urges are like sneaking tiny snacks that are against the diet program to temporarily fill a rumbling tummy. Cravings, on the other hand, are specific desires for something you are not allowed to eat, like barbecued pork ribs or rich chocolate cakes.

Basically, in addiction, urges are needs that arise from wanting to cover or dampen problems, stress, and other emotions whereas cravings root from the memory of the pleasure in taking the substance or in fulfilling the behavior. Therefore, expect these cravings to be more powerful and bending than urges. When these come, expect the worst emotionally and mentally (and physically for substance addicts).

Understand that these cannot be avoided. The best you can hope for is to ride the wave until it subsides – and yes, the feeling will pass. While you're in the middle of it, however, the following are the things you can do:

1. *Engage in an activity.* This can be as simple as reading a book or watching a movie – something that can take your mind to a different place. If, however, the craving is too strong for you to try this, try engaging in something more intense like sports that involve fast movement or exercise. These activities will require focus and attention. At the same time, these will get rid of the "itch" by exhausting your body in a healthy way.

2. *Talk about it.* This is another reason why you will need a friend or family member for support. It's because they'll be the one to do the listening. If you opt for family therapy, these people will be duly informed of what to expect during your recovery, and this is one of the things they can expect. Thus, you are free to express the need, what you feel, and how good it is until the surge subsides. Most hold the idea that speaking about how much you crave for it will only make you want it more. It actually depends because in most cases, recovering addicts unearth more about their condition when they continuously express – they begin to discover the very root of their dependency. And in recovering, this is the most important part of the person's life to understand, because the success of this big change will depend on how well that problem is recognized and addressed.

3. *Urge surf.* There will be times when you'd be caught unprepared by these cravings. You will have no one to talk to, or no option to engage in activities, like during a long solo travel by train or plane. In cases like these, most recovering addicts imagine themselves on top of a large wave, keeping their balance to avoid falling off their boards. The wave will, of course, pass and their main mission is to ride that big crescent of water until it breaks on soft sand. This is why it's called "urge surfing." Difficult waves will come, and you can expect all of them to dissolve into foam; all you need to do is hang on and not to lose your footing.

4. *Fight your thoughts.* This is for the worst of the worst cravings – when you forget all the reasons to stay away from the habit and remember all the pleasures of submitting to it. When this happens, fight the thoughts and try to recall the consequence if you indulge – that you'll essentially be throwing away money that could be better spent on more important things, that you'll break your loved ones' hearts for giving in, and more. Write all of these reasons on a card or a piece of paper then keep it in your wallet or anything that you always bring with you. When these cravings come, this note will be your most potent weapon in fighting it.

The next chapter is for all those who feel that they have lost hope in their battle against addiction and for those who wants a proof that they can overcome every trial that they have faced because of their compulsions.

Chapter 7: When You Feel that You Have Lost Everything

There are a lot of addicts who find that it is pointless for them to recover from their compulsions since they feel that there is nothing left for them to live for. Some feel that they have been aboard a Titanic and that all that is left for them to do is jump into the freezing ocean after all the life boats have sailed away.

What is Left?

When you have lost your job, your family, your home, and your friends because of long-term addiction, or that when you are waiting for a sentence with your hands in handcuffs, you would tend to feel that everything is too late.

However, what is left is the time for you to realize that it is never too late to opt for change. When you've already hit the bottom of the ocean, you would realize that you have nothing left to lose but your addiction. While the effects of your compulsions might have altered your life in the least pleasant way, you have all the reason to embrace change and hope for the better.

Think of all these beautiful things whenever you feel there's nothing worth fighting for or when all hope has been lost:

- Every life on earth is precious and that includes you. Don't think of yourself as nothing but a waste of space.
- If you don't know what your purpose is, know that the rest of the world is also pondering on that same question too.

- No one is better than you. What everyone can do, you can do it too. All it takes are determination and dedication.

- To live is to suffer. You have problems, and so do the people around you. Life is fair that way, and it's how you react to it that decides what will happen to you next.

- If you have nothing more to lose, then that means you have everything to gain.

What You Need to Do

You may realize that things have gotten so bad, but it should not be difficult to take one step at a time towards recovery. You may feel that all hope is lost, but at this point, you need to prove to yourself that life should not always be about desperation and clinging to bad habits just to get over your fears and depression. This is the perfect time for you to understand that once you realize that you are suffering because of addiction, you have the chance to get rid of it.

Again, recovery is a long process, but it pays to start right away. Just take the smallest step that you can now, and then take another step tomorrow. Collectively, all those steps would lead you closer to recovery.

Conclusion

Thank you again for downloading this book!

I hope this book was able to help you understand addiction and recovery, and inspired you to devise the most appropriate way to recover from any compulsive behavior. More importantly, I hope that this book has helped you understand that you need to have that healthy mindset towards change and embrace that commitment.

The next step is to look for a support system that would help you or your loved one recover from addiction, and make sure that you keep your focus on your recovery goals. After committing to resolve addiction, you would also need to see to it that the next actions that you take would bring you closer to living a healthy and holistic life.

If you are currently battling addiction, always keep this book close by. Whenever you forget the reason why you are leading your life to recovery, this book will remind you of that. Whenever you begin blaming yourself for all the heartaches and disappointments you have caused because of the habit, this book will tell you it's not your fault and that it never was. For the times when you think your recovery will mean nothing, for you have already lost everything, this book will tell you your life is worth something, and that it is worth saving.

No life should ever be disregarded, and that includes yours.

Finally, if you enjoyed this book, then I'd like to ask you for a favor, would you be kind enough to leave a review for this book on Amazon? It'd be greatly appreciated!

Thank you and good luck!

Printed in Great Britain
by Amazon